Here I Am, God; Where Are You?

Prayers & Promises For Hospital Patients

John M. Robertson

Tyndale House Publishers, Inc.
Wheaton, Illinois

To all the patients in hospitals
who want to say something to God
but don't know how,
don't feel like it,
or simply
don't want to;
And to those
who want to
and do.
Also, to those
who care for them.

Design by Ted Smith
   Some of the photographs in this book were taken on location at Central
DuPage Hospital, Winfield, Illinois. The publisher gratefully acknowledges
the cooperation of the hospital staff.
   Photography: Beverly Brown—pp. 42, 58 (bottom); William Koech-
ling—p. 28; Fritz Schaeffer—pp. 10-11, 51, 58 (top), 59; Jim Whitmer—pp.
5, 6-7, 15, 36-37.

Library of Congress Catalog Card Number 75-21652. ISBN 8423-1416-4.
Copyright © 1976 by Tyndale House Publishers, Inc.; Wheaton, Illinois
60187. All rights reserved. Tenth printing, September 1980. Printed in the
United States of America.

Preface

Serving as Chaplain at Scottsdale Memorial Hospital, Scottsdale, Arizona, has allowed me to look into the eyes and lives of patients whom words cannot describe. I have tried to put some basic feelings, expressed and unexpressed, into a few simple prayer poems along with some of God's promises from his holy Word.

Unless otherwise identified, the quoted verses are from *The Living Bible*, by permission of Tyndale House Publishers, Wheaton, Illinois.

jmr

Admitting Office

Here I am, God,
    Sitting in the Admitting Office
    Waiting to be admitted.
Here I am
    Feeling so afraid
        And so uncertain
    Filling out forms
        Giving information
    Getting ready
        to turn over my body
    To be examined and probed,
        felt and punched,
        cut and put back together;
    To be used for
        thermometers and needles,
        pills and medicine.
Here I am,
    Feeling worse
    Wanting to be better.
Here I am, God!
    Where are you?

*F*ear not, for I am with you. Do not be dismayed. I am your God. I will strengthen you; I will help you; I will uphold you with my victorious right hand.

Isaiah 41:10

I am leaving you with a gift—peace of mind and heart! And the peace I give isn't fragile like the peace the world gives. So don't be troubled or afraid.

John 14:27

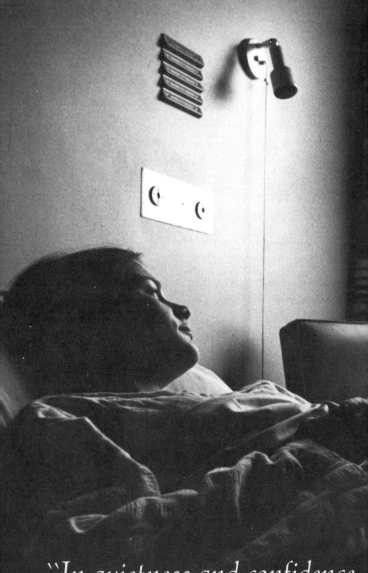

"In quietness and confidence
is your strength"

A. M.

It's busy this morning, Lord;
    Lots of activity
    Lots of noise;
        Breakfast trays
          Bedpans
            Baths
        Changing beds
          Checking temperatures
        Telephones ringing
          Loudspeakers shouting
            Carts crashing!
        Patients going for
          Operations
            X-rays
              Therapies
                Dismissals

        Doctors calling
          and being called;
        Nurses coming
          and going;
And God,
    I hurt!
        I want quiet
          and peace!

*F*or the Lord God, the Holy One of Israel, says: Only in returning to me and waiting for me will you be saved; in quietness and confidence is your strength.

Isaiah 30:15

*B*e still, and know that I am God. I am exalted among the nations, I am exalted in the earth!

Psalm 46:10, RSV

I have told you all this so that you will have peace of heart and mind. Here on earth you will have many trials and sorrows; but cheer up, for I have overcome the world.

John 16:33

Thanks, Lord,...

for food to eat

Mealtime

Why is it, Lord,
That between meals
I get so hungry
But when I see food
I don't care to eat?
Sometimes I even
Have my choice of menus;
Other times I can't get
What I want.
O Lord!
Help me to be grateful
for what I get
Be it too little
or too much;
of one thing
or the other.
Thanks, Lord,
for food to eat;
Just give me a better appetite
to enjoy it.

*S*o my counsel is: Don't worry about
things—food, drink, and clothes. For you
already have life and a body—and they are
far more important than what to eat and
wear. Look at the birds! They don't worry
about what to eat—they don't need to sow
or reap or store up food—for your heavenly
Father feeds them. And you are far more
valuable to him than they are. Will all
your worries add a single moment to
your life?

Matthew 6:25-27

*F*or everything God made is good, and
we may eat it gladly if we are thankful
for it, and if we ask God to bless it,
for it is made good by the Word of God
and prayer.

1 Timothy 4:4, 5

*B*lessed are those who hunger and thirst
for righteousness, for they shall be
satisfied.

Matthew 5:6, RSV

Visiting Hours

O God,
Sometimes I don't feel
Like I want any visitors,
Especially those I hardly know,
Who only come to see you
When you are sick!
I just want to be
Left alone
to relax
to read
to rest.
Solitude can be meaningful
To mental
emotional
and physical health.
And yet I want
My family
and friends
to visit
Because I know what
Loneliness does too!
It can hurt—
Like pain.
God—
Make me happy
To see my visitors.

*C*ontinue to love each other with true brotherly love. Don't forget to be kind to strangers, for some who have done this have entertained angels without realizing it!

Hebrews 13:1, 2

*T*he fear of the Lord leads to life; and he who has it rests satisfied; he will not be visited by harm.

Proverbs 19:23, RSV

Pain

I hurt, God;
Oh how I hurt!
My body aches,
I feel sore all over.
Pills and shots
Don't seem to help.
Even to change position
Sends pangs of pain.
Is there any purpose
In suffering, God?
Does pain have
any reason for being?
If there is any lesson
to be learned,
Help me to learn it, God.
Otherwise, take away the pain
or send some relief.

I waited patiently for God to help me;
then he listened and heard my cry. He
lifted me out of the pit of despair, out
from the bog and the mire, and set my
feet on a hard, firm path and steadied
me as I walked along. He has given me a
new song to sing, of praises to our God.
Now many will hear of the glorious things
he did for me, and stand in awe before
the Lord, and put their trust in him.
Many blessings are given to those who
trust the Lord, and have no confidence
in those who are proud, or who trust
in idols.

Psalm 40:1-4

I heard a loud shout from the throne
saying, "Look, the home of God is now
among men, and he will live with them
and they will be his people; yes, God
himself will be among them. He will wipe
away all tears from their eyes, and there
shall be no more death, nor sorrow, nor
crying, nor pain. All of that has gone
forever."

Revelation 21:3, 4

Your Workmanship

is Marvelous

X-ray

The semidarkness
    is depressing, Lord.
"Take a deep breath"
"You may breathe now"
    "Turn on your right side"
    "Turn on your left side"
        "Now on your stomach"
        "Now on your back"
I'm not feeling that well, God.
    In fact, I feel pretty sick.
Why do they have to look
    at everything inside me?
How much longer, Lord?
    What will they find?
    What do they expect to find?
    What do they want to find?
How long will I have to wait
    Before they tell me?
O God,
    Let the pictures come out
    and let there be
                Nothing!

O Lord, you have examined my heart and know everything about me. You know when I sit or stand. When far away you know my every thought. . . . You made all the delicate, inner parts of my body, and knit them together in my mother's womb. Thank you for making me so wonderfully complex! It is amazing to think about. Your workmanship is marvelous—and how well I know it. You were there while I was being formed in utter seclusion! You saw me before I was born and scheduled each day of my life before I began to breathe. Every day was recorded in your Book! How precious it is, Lord, to realize that you are thinking about me constantly!

Psalm 139:1, 2, 13-17

Surgery

Lying on a cart
Staring at a ceiling
Going down an elevator
Being pushed down the corridor
        O God,
                Couldn't a better means
                        of transportation
                Have been invented
                        to take a body
                        to surgery?
The sterilized sanctuary
        Where masked priests
        Quietly perform their ritual
                in hushed whispers
        And finger their instruments
                in calm readiness
                and anticipation.
O God,
        Steady the doctor's hands
                And use him to heal
                        my diseased body.
I'm scared, God;
        I fight the drowsiness
                that overcomes me.
Let me relax
        in the knowledge
        of your knowledge about me.

*G*ive your burdens to the Lord. He will carry them. He will not permit the godly to slip or fall.

Psalm 55:22

*L*et him have all your worries and cares, for he is always thinking about you and watching everything that concerns you.

1 Peter 5:7

After Visiting Hours

I am alone, God.
   Family and friends
      have come and gone;
   The corridors
      grow empty and still;
   The nurses have finished
      their routine room checks;
   The lights are dimmed
      and the room is darkened;
And I am alone.
   The long night hours
      are before me;
   The unknown outcome
      of today's tests
      frightens me;
   It is difficult to sleep
      but more difficult
      to stay awake.
O God, I am alone.

God will never let me stumble, slip, or fall. For he is always watching, never sleeping. Jehovah himself is caring for you! He is your defender. He protects you day and night. He keeps you from all evil, and preserves your life. He keeps his eye upon you . . . and always guards you.

Psalm 121:3-8

Impatience

O God!
   I'm an impatient patient today.
   Nothing seems to go right.
      I rang
         But the nurse didn't come;
      I asked
         But received no answers.
   The doctor
      doesn't tell me
         what's wrong;
   The nurses
      don't tell me
         when I can go home.
      Medication is given
         but I don't know why;
      Consultation is going on
         but I don't know how
            I'm doing!
Does anyone care, God?
   Does anyone really care?

*D*on't be impatient. Wait for the Lord, and he will come and save you! Be brave, stouthearted and courageous. Yes, wait and he will help you.

Psalm 27:14

*B*ut they that wait upon the Lord shall renew their strength. They shall mount up with wings like eagles; they shall run and not be weary; they shall walk and not faint.

Isaiah 40:31

He will make me smile again

for he is my God

Depression

Depression has hit me, God.
    All joy has gone from me.
      Despair
             Disappointment
                    Disillusionment
                        rule the day
    I hurt from the skin in
      I have knots in my stomach
        I feel weighted down
    I want to
        hit!
                move!
                    strike!
                      run!
But I can't
    I'm welded to the bed.
O God!
    Help me—
        Help me
            to see
            to sense
    Your peace
        and presence;
    Give me hope
        in the midst
            of my depression.

O *my soul, don't be discouraged. Don't be upset. Expect God to act! For I know that I shall again have plenty of reason to praise him for all that he will do. He is my help! He is my God!*

Psalm 42:11

O *my soul, why be so gloomy and discouraged? Trust in God! I shall again praise him for his wondrous help; he will make me smile again,* for he is my God!

Psalm 43:5

Thanksgiving

I feel much better today, Lord,
And I'm thankful!
I want to thank you
for being with me
during this sickness,
for the doctors and nurses
who cared for me,
for giving them
knowledge
wisdom
and patience
to help me
in my recovery.
Thank you, too, Lord,
for friends
who remembered
who helped
who visited
who prayed.
And thank you
for the lessons learned
while here in the hospital—
that I cannot trust in
wealth or health,
that life is
so short and so uncertain,
that only you

are eternal and sure
and that no other refuge
have I but you.
Thank you, Lord!

*Seventy years are given us! And some may
even live to eighty. But even the best
of these years are often emptiness and
pain; soon they disappear, and we are
gone. . . . Teach us to number our
days and recognize how few they are;
help us to spend them as we should.*

Psalm 90:10, 12

*Always give thanks for everything to our
God and Father in the name of our
Lord Jesus Christ.*

Ephesians 5:20

*It is good to say, "Thank you" to the
Lord, to sing praises to the God who
is above all gods. Every morning tell him,
"Thank you for your kindness," and
every evening rejoice in all his
faithfulness.*

Psalm 92:1, 2

Chapel

The stillness
      of a sanctuary—
The peacefulness
      of the hospital chapel!
It's a great place
      to be with you, God,
To sit in silence
         To whisper my deepest needs
                  To tell you how I feel
                        To thank you for your love
            To listen for your voice
                        To know that I don't have
                        to face my crisis alone.
The assurance
      and reassurance
            that comes from
Your Word
      and the hymns—
I need this, Lord.
      Thank you
            for being here.

*C*ome, kneel before the Lord our Maker,
for he is our God. We are his sheep and
he is our Shepherd. Oh, that you would
hear him calling you today and come to
him!

Psalm 95:6, 7

*D*on't worry about anything; instead, pray
about everything; tell God your needs
and don't forget to thank him for his
answers.

Philippians 4:6

*P*ray all the time. Ask God for anything
in line with the Holy Spirit's wishes.
Plead with him, reminding him of your
needs, and keep praying earnestly for all
Christians everywhere.

Ephesians 6:18

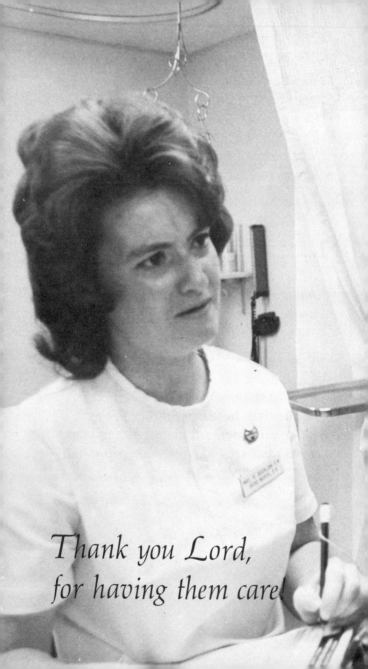

Thank you Lord,
for having them care!

Doctors

Are these men
    real, God?
        They look!
        They examine!
        They test!
        They probe!
    Sometimes
        they blink
            and nod;
    But they don't
            say much.
Even when I ask
    I get
        evasive answers
            or
        mysterious looks
            and
    I can't help
        wondering!
O God,
    I know I need
        to trust my doctor
    But I would like
        to know what my problem is.
    Can't we
        stop playing games
            and
        be honest with each other?

God,
    help my doctor
        to tell me the truth
           and
    help me
        to accept it.

Jesus said to them, "You are truly my disciples if you live as I tell you to, and you will know the truth, and the truth will set you free."

John 8:31b, 32

For I know the plans I have for you, says the Lord. They are plans for good and not for evil, to give you a future and a hope. In those days when you pray, I will listen. You will find me when you seek me, if you look for me in earnest.

Jeremiah 29:11-13

Nurses

Angels of mercy
or disturbers of the peace?
They are your angels, God!
When I grumble,
They smile!
When I complain,
They serve!
When I hurt,
They help!
I know I'm not always
pleasant to them
and yet
expect them
to be
pleasant to me.
Help me, God,
to remember that
they are doing their best
to make me feel
at my best.
Thank you, Lord,
for having them care!

*A*dmit your faults to one another and pray for each other so that you may be healed. The earnest prayer of a righteous man has great power and wonderful results.

James 5:16

*D*ear brothers, I am not writing out a new rule for you to obey, for it is an old one you have always had, right from the start. You have heard it all before. Yet it is always new, and works for you just as it did for Christ; and as we obey this commandment, to love one another, the darkness in our lives disappears and the new light of life in Christ shines in.

1 John 2:7, 8

I will not be afraid ...

for you are close

Cancer

"Cancer!"
>> That word that cuts
>>> like a surgeon's scalpel.
Cancer!
>> O God, can it be true?
>> O God, can there be any escape?
I need you now
>> more than ever before,
>>> Lord.
>> Don't leave me alone;
>>> don't forsake me.
I don't know
>> if there is any hope.
I don't know
>> what the future will be
>>> or
>> how long the future will be.
But God!
>> By your presence
>> and
>> In your love
Help me not to be afraid.

*F*or God has said, "I will never, never fail you nor forsake you." That is why we can say without any doubt or fear, "The Lord is my Helper and I am not afraid of anything that mere man can do to me."

Hebrews 13:5b, 6

*E*ven when walking through the dark valley of death I will not be afraid, for you are close beside me, guarding, guiding all the way.

Psalm 23:4

The Emergency Room

The Emergency Room! O God!
     This is the place
          Where someone brings someone else
               Because of tragedy.
     But not to me—
          Always to someone else!
     Yet here I am
          And it's scary; it's frightening
          And I'm afraid!
This is the place
     Where nurses and doctors
          Half run, half walk;
     Where ambulances hurry to a halt
     And doors fly open
          And carts roll by.
     Where a world of
          Dizziness, confusion, and pain
               Blurs the world of reality.
O God,
     I don't mean to use you
          As a heavenly life-guard
          To be called upon for rescue
     But I need you now.

I want you to trust me in your times
of trouble, so I can rescue you, and
you can give me glory.

Psalm 50:15b

*T*he Lord is good. When trouble comes,
he is the place to go! And he knows
everyone who trusts him!

Nahum 1:7

Accident

I'm awake now, Lord.
They have
picked out the pieces of glass,
sewn up the cuts,
put casts on the broken bones.
How quickly
the routine of life
is altered;
How swiftly
I need to reorient
my life-style.
O Lord!
One moment—
the picture of health
The next—
helpless in a hospital.
Why, God, why?
It doesn't make sense
There is no rhyme
nor reason
There is no
figuring it out.
Where are you, God?
Are you in this with me?

*T*rust in the Lord with all your heart,
and do not rely on your own insight.
In all your ways acknowledge him, and
he will make straight your paths. Be not
wise in your own eyes; fear the Lord,
and turn away from evil. It will be
healing to your flesh and refreshment
to your bones.

Proverbs 3:5-8, RSV

*A*nd we know that all that happens to
us is working for our good if we love
God and are fitting into his plans.

Romans 8:28

The pain forgotten ...

The anxiety gone ...

O. B.

O God!
>   The pain was awful!
>   The anxiety was overwhelming!
>>   Would I make it?
>>   Would my baby be all right?
>   And then it was over
>   Delivering and being delivered
>>   The pain forgotten
>>   The anxiety gone
>>>   At the sight
>>>   Of my newborn!

O God!
>   What perfection
>   What beauty
>>   All fingers and toes
>>>   Accounted for
>>   And a cry
>>>   That's a song
>>>   To a mother's ear.

O God!
>   Thank you.

When a woman is in travail she has sorrow, because her hour has come; but when she is delivered of the child, she no longer remembers the anguish, for joy that a child is born into the world.

John 16:21, RSV

Nursery

Life!
    O God! when does it begin?
        Those little bodies
            so perfectly formed
            yet so utterly helpless
            and so completely dependent.
    But God!
        Though we don't know when
            physical life
                begins
        We know that
            eternal life
                begins
        With a personal confession
            of you
                as Lord and Savior.
Help me, O God,
    To help my child
        To know and love
YOU!

*J*esus (said), "What I am telling you so earnestly is this: Unless one is born of water and the Spirit, he cannot enter the Kingdom of God. Men can only reproduce human life, but the Holy Spirit gives new life from heaven; so don't be surprised at my statement that you must be born again!"

John 3:5-7

*T*each a child to choose the right path, and when he is older he will remain upon it.

Proverbs 22:6

Pediatrics

Children, O God,
Children!
 Who are
   so small
     so scared
       so wide-eyed
         so wondering!
 To whom
   the world is so big,
   the hospital so strange,
   medical instruments
    so terrifying,
   doctors and nurses
    so threatening.
Bless them, Lord,
 Bless the children!
 Take away their fears;
 Give them an extra dose
  of simple faith;
 Help them to trust
  those who care for them;
 Make them aware
  of your healing presence.

*J*esus said, "Let the little children come
to me, and don't prevent them. For of
such is the Kingdom of Heaven."

Matthew 19:14

*J*esus called a small child over to him
and set the little fellow down among them,
and said, "Unless you turn to God from
your sins and become as little children,
you will never get into the Kingdom
of Heaven."

Matthew 18:2

So wide-eyed

        so wondering

Special Care Unit

This is a foreboding place, Lord,
 Shut off from
  the rest of the world.
This is where life
 Hangs in a balance
  midst monitors
  and machines
  and tubes
  and needles
   of seemingly
   every size
   and description
  to keep one alive
  to restore to health.
It's a frightening place, Lord,
 because one feels
  so helpless
   so alone.
But it's a good place
 because they watch so carefully
 and they care so tenderly.
And here I am, God!
 Are you here, too?

*We live within the shadow of the Almighty,
sheltered by the God who is above all
gods. This I declare, that he alone is my
refuge, my place of safety; he is my God,
and I am trusting him. For he rescues
you from every trap, and protects you
from the fatal plague. He will shield you
with his wings! They will shelter you.
His faithful promises are your armor.
Now you don't need to be afraid of the
dark any more, nor fear the dangers
of the day.*

Psalm 91:1-5

Going Home

Going home!
Yes, God,
I got the news today.
The doctor told me,
"You can go home."
Those words are better medicine
than any that comes
in a bottle.
But they were too long
in coming, God.
I don't know
how long eternity is
but it seemed like it here.
Thanks, God,
for seeing me through
for giving me the courage
for granting me more time
for giving me a new lease on life
for allowing me to face
the world of health
as I faced
the world of sickness.
Here I am, God!
Where are you?
I'm going home!
Are you going with me?

*J*esus) told his disciples, "I have been given all authority in heaven and earth. Therefore go and make disciples in all the nations, baptizing them into the name of the Father and of the Son and of the Holy Spirit, and then teach these new disciples to obey all the commands I have given you; and be sure of this— that I am with you always, even to the end of the world."

Matthew 28:18-20

*L*et not your heart be troubled. You are trusting God, now trust in me. There are many homes up there where my Father lives, and I am going to prepare them for your coming. When everything is ready, then I will come and get you, so that you can always be with me where I am. If this weren't so, I would tell you plainly.

John 14:1-3